PRAISE FOR STORY SELLING

"Harry Maziar is one of the greatest salesmen of all time. He always knew his customer and knew that to keep the customer, he had to fulfill every promise he made. And he did it with humor and intelligence. Story Selling is the print version of Harry Maziar."

Bernie Marcus

Co-founder, The Home Depot, and Chairman,
The Marcus Foundation

"Stories speak louder than words, and Harry Maziar is a great story teller! His collection of stories and real-life experiences provides important insights from a master salesman and more than a few chuckles along the way. In any job or relationship, we are called upon to 'sell,' and Maziar's advice will benefit each of us."

Kelly N. Stanley

Former Chairman, United States Chamber of Commerce
and Retired CEO, Cardinal Health System, Inc.

"Sales, like story telling, is an art — part thought, part inspiration. Harry Maziar has simplified the art of selling stories to paint by numbers. Each story paints a picture and builds a skill in the reader's mind; each lesson is easy to understand and entertaining to read. Story Selling is a must read for the Atlanta Hawks sales team!"

Steve Kooni

CEO, NBA Atlanta Hawks a

"Few know selling — or understand its concepts, skills and techniques — better than Harry Maziar. Even fewer can write about it with his combination of charm, humor and grace. Through stories, Harry reminds us that selling, like life, is about building meaningful relationships. When we help others accomplish their dreams, ours are fulfilled as well. Story Selling shares powerful 'hints' of wisdom gleaned from a life of selling."

Kathy S. Schwaig, PhD

Dean, Michael J. Coles College of Business,

Kennesaw State University

STORY STELLING

STORY SELLING

Sage Advice and Common Sense About Sales and Success

HARRY MAZIAR

NEW YORK

NASHVILLE • MELBOURNE • VANCOUVER

STORY SELLING
Sage Advice and Common Sense About Sales and Success

© 2018 Harry Maziar

Published in New York, New York, by Morgan James Publishing. Morgan James is a trademark of Morgan James, LLC. www.MorganJamesPublishing.com

The Morgan James Speakers Group can bring authors to your live event. For more information or to book an event visit The Morgan James Speakers Group at www.TheMorganJamesSpeakersGroup.com.

ISBN 978-1-68350-410-8 paperback
ISBN 978-1-68350-411-5 eBook
Library of Congress Control Number: 2017900573

Cover Design by:
Megan Whitney
megan@creativeninjadesigns.com

Interior Design by:
Chris Treccani
www.3dogdesign.net

In an effort to support local communities, raise awareness and funds, Morgan James Publishing donates a percentage of all book sales for the life of each book to Habitat for Humanity Peninsula and Greater Williamsburg.

Get involved today! Visit
www.MorganJamesBuilds.com

TABLE OF CONTENTS

vii

Stories touch the human spirit.

FOREWORD

Once upon a time, there was...

Notice what happens when you read these words. If you're like most people, your immediate response is: "There was... what?" Your imagination is already stirring. There's a sense of anticipation. You want to know more. Just a few words disarmed your resident skeptic and aroused your curiosity. And in just a few words, I've captured your attention and put you in a state of receptivity for whatever message I am about to give you in the form of a story. That's why the art of storytelling is an essential skill for absolutely everyone. Storytelling is, without a doubt, the easiest and most effective form of communication virtually anyone can use to inform, inspire, promote, enroll, market or sell. Storytelling is an exceptional vehicle for building credibility, engendering greater customer loyalty, and presenting a highly compelling offer.

Stories engage the reader's emotions and spirit. A good story invites the reader in, and they then become an active participant and co-creator – not necessarily in the words of the story itself, but in the inner experience, and the meaningful translation into one's own self.

In *Story Selling*, readers learn the power of this highly influential vehicle of expression and involvement to the art and science of marketing. Harry Maziar is a master storyteller. You will be educated, encouraged, inspired and entertained with his current, relevant message. Be prepared.

David L. Hancock
Founder, Morgan James Publishing

Stories Speak Louder Than Words

I've been selling my entire life.

It all started with a front-yard Coca-Cola stand. I was hooked. Then, it was on to selling peanuts at Bobby Dodd Stadium at Grant Field. As a young teenager, my repertoire expanded to shirts and shoes. When I got a bit older, I sold football colors and pennants in Atlanta and on some weekends took a bus to the University of Tennessee in Knoxville where there was less competition. That's where I learned the importance of asking for the order.

After short stints selling insurance and groceries, I spent a career at Zep Manufacturing Company, first as a sales rep and later as Director of Sales. Then, for many years, I had the honor of leading more than 2,000 salespeople as president of the company. I had a rewarding and fulfilling career and was blessed to do something that I loved every day. That's the very best advice I can give: do something you love.

Some might say that selling industrial cleaning products like waxes, cleaners, car wash, degreasers, disinfectants and thousands of other formulations is not that critical. To that I would respond, "Selling Zep products is not a life-and-death matter…it's much more important than that."

After a lifetime in sales, I'd like to think I've learned a thing or two. I've certainly learned that selling is much more than explaining features and benefits, overcoming objections and closing. It's about caring, building relationships and fulfilling customers' expectations, aspirations and dreams. In spite of the occasional bad press, no job is more important than sales.

An especially meaningful lesson I learned over the past half century is that the best salespeople use stories to sell. They paint pictures with words…pictures that create feelings, excitement and action. Stories are a persuasive sales tool. They often speak louder and are more relatable than all of the sales lingo you can muster.

Simply said, the more stories you tell…the more you sell.

Stories are also a powerful learning tool. Rudyard Kipling once said, "If history was taught in the form of stories, it would never be forgotten." For more than 27 years, I wrote a weekly sales letter to "the team" about the concepts, skills and techniques that would make them better salespeople. These weekly letters included (you guessed it) stories about my and other sales reps' personal experiences, articles I had clipped and filed, and pieces of wisdom I'd picked up along the way. Each sales letter ended with a "Harry's Hint" – a short, helpful thought or suggestion.

This book is a collection of 50 of my favorite hints, each expanded into a story** that teaches a key selling principle. The stories are humorous and memorable; the lessons valuable and timeless. Together, they lay the foundation for success, not just in sales but in life.

No one can be certain that the stories you're about to read will teach you a thing. But, like chicken soup, they can't hurt. What I do know is that they made me think, and if they do the same for you, then "you're gaining on it." I hope they will give you greater confidence, help you make friends and relate to others, keep you motivated or just make you smile. You can also use them as conversation or meeting starters with your sales team.

You may be familiar with some of the vignettes and anecdotes I've included. It's been said that there's really nothing new under the sun. So, the question is…if you're already familiar with the stories and lessons, are you applying them?

Just because we know what to do doesn't mean we do it. Your success will be determined not by what you read and learn, but by what you do with what you learn.

When you finish this little book, I encourage you to pay your sales success forward by sharing your favorite selling stories and experiences with me at harrymaziar@gmail.com. Together, we'll create *Story Selling 2* and make a difference in the science, art and fun of professional selling.

I have benefited tremendously over the years from the commitments and talents of so many people who have brought honor to the profession of selling. In my own effort to "pay it forward," I am contributing half of the profits from this book to charity. (Make that 49 percent…a good salesperson always has control. Oh, what the heck! Let's make it 100 percent for the benefit of charity!)

As they have done for me, I hope these stories and lessons will help you be even better at what you do each day.

Good luck and good selling.

Harry

**I have tried in good faith and with all due diligence – sometimes successfully and sometimes not – to find the original sources of the stories and anecdotes that are not my own. A good salesperson always gives credit where credit is due. If you know the source of a story, please contact me at harrymaziar@gmail.com so that I may give the author due credit.

CHAPTER 1

There's a Mighty Big Difference Between Good, Sound Reasons and Reasons That Sound Good

One day years ago as my day was ending, I called my wife and asked, "What's for dinner?"

"What would you like?" she responded.

As it was already 7 p.m., I astutely concluded that I was bringing dinner home that night. We settled on fried chicken, and off I headed to one of the local chains.

At the restaurant, I ordered my chicken, drove to the pickup window and paid. Just as I was about to drive out, I noticed a sign advertising hot biscuits for 35 cents each or $1.50 for half a dozen. Not able to resist a bargain, I decided to order half a dozen.

No one was behind me, so I backed up to the window and gave the young lady my order. A minute or two later, she returned to inform me that the biscuits were in the oven cooking and that it would be about 10 minutes before they were ready. A glance at my watch told me it was getting late, so I told her I'd better pass and head on home.

She then mentioned that they had five biscuits available, but not the half dozen. Happy that I would get some biscuits after all, I said I'd take the five. She returned with a sack of biscuits and said, "That will be $1.75."

"There must be some mistake," I said. "If they are $1.50 for half a dozen, surely five couldn't cost $1.75."

With a somewhat perplexed look on her face, she responded, "Yes, the price is $1.75, because if you don't buy six, they are 35 cents each."

"I do want to buy six, but you don't have them ready," I said. "You can't charge me more for five than you would for six."

Not to be deterred, she said, "Yes, sir, it will be $1.75."

I bit my lip, said a few choice words under my breath and asked if I could speak to the manager. When the manager appeared in the window, I explained that I had wanted six biscuits, that they only had five ready, and that his employee wanted me to pay more for the five than for the six I originally ordered.

He heard me out, thought for a moment, and said, "Yes, sir, it will be $1.75. If you don't buy half a dozen, then they are 35 cents each."

I knew I was in trouble with a capital T (for either Temper or Trauma). I thought for a moment and then said, mustering my best salesmanship, "Sell me six biscuits for $1.50, and you can owe me one. I'll pick up the other one tomorrow."

He agreed, I assume thinking he had won the battle. Needless to say, I didn't go back for my biscuit, and I've never been back for any more chicken.

Is the customer always right? Not necessarily. But there is an ever-growing group of failed salespeople who make a habit of winning the battle and losing the war.

There is an old adage that says, "The boss may not always be right, but he or she is always the boss." Likewise, the customer

may not always be right, but he or she is always the customer...
if respected, treated right, cared for and helped.

The primary responsibility of a business is to give customers what *they* want, not what *we* want. Successful salespeople have learned this valuable lesson. They impart confidence, comfort and, most importantly, confirmation that the choices their customers make are the correct ones.

Good selling consists of selling goods that won't come back to customers who will.

Many have said that there is a thin line between comedy and tragedy, and in my mind, this biscuit story crosses that line. Always remember that there is a big difference between good, sound reasons and reasons that just sound good.

Harry's Hint

Don't let what you are doing get to you before you get to it.

2

An Investment in Knowledge Always Pays Interest

One of my favorite stories is about a father who, on a cloudy and threatening afternoon, took his young son out for a walk. As they strolled along, the youngster, with typical childlike curiosity, asked his father, "How does the electricity go through those wires stretched between the power poles?"

"I don't know," his father replied. "I never knew much about electricity."

A few blocks farther on, observing the darkening sky, the boy asked another question. "What causes lightning and thunder?"

"To tell the truth," said the father, "I never exactly understood that myself."

The boy continued to ask questions throughout the walk, none of which his father could answer. With the rain now imminent, they hurried home. As they started up the front steps, the son turned and said, "Pop, I hope you don't mind me asking so many questions."

"Of course not," replied the father. "How else are you going to learn?"

As a professional salesperson, you can say too much, but you can't know too much. Knowledge is part and parcel of your "inventory," and it needs to be constantly updated.

The best way to become an old dog is to stop learning new tricks.

Successful salespeople keep learning. But for how long? The Roman philosopher Seneca (4BC to 65AD) said, "You should keep on learning as long as there is something you do not know." What great advice for every salesperson.

Keep your eyes and ears open. Be inquisitive…ask questions. Don't assume…find out.

What you don't know won't help you.

Just Because It's Common Sense Doesn't Make It Common Practice

It's a challenge to remember – and even more importantly, to practice – the basics of selling every day. We start with good intentions, but too often complacency finds its way into our daily efforts. Inevitably, we begin to coast and then there's only one place to go...downhill.

Here's a story about a salesperson who forgot the basics and the resulting consequences.

An elderly couple hadn't bought a new refrigerator in 30 years, and the appliance salesman was extolling the features of his deluxe model. The couple seemed impressed, but they told him they had promised his competitor across the street that they would stop by and see what he had to offer. This didn't worry the salesman because he knew that his competitor carried the same brand but at a higher price. The couple left, promising to return if the other store had nothing they liked better.

A while later, the couple returned and told the salesman they had bought a refrigerator from his competitor. Mustering a smile, the salesman told them he was glad they had found what they wanted.

"By the way, which model did you buy?" the salesman asked.

The elderly gentleman read the model number from his sales slip.

A bit exasperated, the salesman replied, "But that's the same model I showed you, and mine sells for $50 less!

"It couldn't be the same model," the woman said. "The one we bought has a little light inside that turns on when you open the door."

"All refrigerators have that," the salesman replied.

"Really?" the woman said. "Then why didn't you tell us yours had it?"

Ouch!

If you don't drop the ball, you won't have to complain about the way it bounces.

Never assume too much. Don't take anything for granted. Tell the whole story. Remember that features and benefits coupled with passion and professionalism keep your "light" on as you "light up" your customers' interest.

4

The Most Important Thing About Goals... Is to Have One

Years ago, I read a true story about Florence Chadwick, who set out to swim 26 miles from Santa Catalina Island off the coast of Los Angeles to the California mainland – something no woman had ever done.

Florence trained for months for the challenge. When the big day came, she slipped into the icy waters and began the slow, rhythmic stroke she had diligently practiced to utilize her energy to the utmost.

At first, she felt extremely confident, but as the hours wore on, she grew weak in the cold water. A fog rolled in, making conditions worse. Eventually the fog became so thick she had to get directions from the crew on board the boat that was following her in case something went wrong.

"A little to the left," a crew member yelled through a hand-held loudspeaker. "A little to the right," he shouted again when she veered off course.

This went on for hours. Finally, Florence could take no more. Despairingly, she begged to be pulled out of the freezing water, just one mile from shore. Over 95 percent of the distance had been achieved, yet she failed.

After a few cups of hot tea, she explained that she couldn't keep going when there was no goal in sight. "If I could have seen the shore, I would have made it."

What a fundamental principle of sales success. Without a goal, you will find yourself adrift, just like Florence. If you don't know where you're going, you will certainly get there. You may have the best training, a good market and the right tools, but without a purpose, a destination – a GOAL – all your efforts and hard work will be for naught.

Goal setting is an integral and necessary part of success. Very little that is truly meaningful is ever accomplished without a goal. Are your goals clearly defined? If not, begin with a clear-cut, well-defined objective.

Then move forward with determination, grit, focus, passion and good, old-fashioned hard work. Very few geniuses or superstars talk about their "gift"; rather, they talk about their commitment, hard work and long hours.

By the way, two months after her failed attempt, Florence tried her epic swim again. Once again, the fog was so thick she couldn't see land. But this time, she later explained, she kept a mental image of the shoreline in her mind. Not only did she achieve her goal, she beat the men's record time by two hours!

Goals and hard work...an unbeatable combination.

5

"I Must Do Something" Will Always Solve More Problems Than "Something Must Be Done"

In the biblical story of David and Goliath, a young Israelite slays the Philistine giant. The King of Israel and all his army were too afraid to fight Goliath. They said, "He is so big, we can never kill him."

Young David volunteered to fight. He looked at the same giant and thought, "He is so big, I can't miss him."

What an attitude!

How do you face your "giant" problems? Just as David did...

Be bold, fearless, resolute and confident.

Look for a weakness and take advantage of the opportunity. David found a hole in Goliath's armor with his very first shot. But remember...David chose five smooth stones for his shepherd's bag. If his first shot hadn't hit the mark, he had more at the ready.

Yes, a positive attitude and confidence go a long way.

Successful people also know they need to have a "Plan B." Even the NBA's best know the importance of rebounding— following up a missed shot.

Life and selling are not perfect. Be prepared to act and react. Be ready and willing to do *something*, just as David did. And always be ready with extra stones...just in case.

6

The Nice Thing About Teamwork Is That You Always Have Others on Your Side

Years ago, life was simpler. The factory whistle, the drug store lunch counter and the town square were a part of daily life. So much has changed in today's fast-paced world. Yet so many life lessons from yesteryear are just as relevant today as they were then. This is one of those lessons.

There was a man who lived in a small town. Each day at five minutes before noon, he would call the telephone company and ask what time it was. Each time, he got the same operator and received the same answer: "Five minutes before 12 o'clock."

The caller never left his name, nor did the operator ask why he made it a practice to call at the same time to ask the same question every day. (It was against company policy for operators to engage callers in conversation.) This ritual went on for 25 years.

Finally, on the day the operator was to retire, the man called as usual. This time, the operator couldn't resist asking the question she'd had for so long. "Why have you called each day for 25 years and asked what time it is?"

"Well, I work at the factory in town," came the answer. "It's my responsibility to blow the whistle to announce that it is 12 noon. I've called you each day at five minutes before noon to be certain I had the time right."

"Well, what do you know about that!" said the operator. "All these years, I've used the sound of that whistle at noontime to get the correct time to set our clocks by."

How dramatically this story demonstrates how much we all need each other…how much we are dependent upon each other for success.

There are those who say that selling is the original do-it-yourself profession. You are out there by yourself, and when the spotlight shines on you, you'd better be up for the performance.

But I also believe no one achieves success totally on his or her own. I'm not sure it takes a village, but I'm certain it takes a team. It takes the coordination and dedication of many people for any salesperson to succeed. Even the Lone Ranger had Tonto.

Don't ever take for granted your purchasing department, manufacturing and production people, warehouse and customer service support teams, various administrators and the host of others who are behind the scenes pulling for you to get that next order. Be aware of those who support you.

Better yet…every chance you get, let them know of your appreciation.

Together, in the spirit of cooperation and with singleness of purpose, there is no limit to what can be accomplished.

Harry's Hint

Most of the footprints in the sands of time were made by work shoes.

Good Enough Never Is

I often tell the story about a teenage boy who went into his neighborhood drugstore and made a call on their phone. (Clearly, this was well before cell phones.) When the call was answered, the boy asked, "Do you need a stock boy?"

"No, we already have one," the party on the other end of the line said.

"Is his work satisfactory?" the boy persisted. "Yes, his work is excellent," came the reply.

"Thank you," said the boy, and he hung up the phone.

The puzzled druggist, overhearing this conversation, said, "I thought your mother told me you already have a job."

"I do," the boy said proudly. "Those were the people I work for. I was just checking up on myself."

All successful people share this attitude. They are proud of the work they do and, in turn, checkup on it regularly. They know...

If better is possible, good is not enough.

8

Don't Count the Words . . .
Make the Words Count

I once asked one of my salespeople how many calls he had made that day.

"Sixty," he responded.

I was shocked and asked how he could have made so many calls.

"It was no big deal," he said. "I would have made more, but someone stopped me to ask what I was selling."

Cute…but not the way to fame and fortune.

That story reminds me of the farmer from down south who arrived home after attending a political rally in town.

"Who spoke?" asked his wife. "The mayor," replied the farmer.

"What did he talk about?"

"Well," the man said, scratching his head, "he didn't say."

Make sure that is not the reaction to your sales calls. Have a point to get to…then get to it quickly.

Being long-winded can have its merits though. There once was a young attorney who showed little aptitude for the law and even less for public speaking, but neither handicap prevented him from pursuing a career as a criminal attorney. Finally, the day came for him to argue his first murder case. He asked a colleague in his firm to attend his closing argument.

Halfway through his summation, our aspiring Perry Mason slipped a note to the other attorney: "How am I doing?"

"Keep talking," the other lawyer wrote. "The longer you talk, the longer he lives." [i]

These three anecdotes have one common theme: Success in whatever you do depends on the communication process.

You can talk too long or not long enough…it depends on what you have to say and how you say it. As salespeople, we make our living with words. Be sure you communicate clearly, concisely, effectively and emphatically.

While quantity helps, quality is the real answer.

Don't count your words…make your words count.

9

If You Are Angling for Success, the Most Important Angle is the Try-Angle

Mickey Rooney, who died in 2014, was a star of stage and screen. His career spanned 90 years, and he appeared in more than 300 films. He could do it all: sing, dance and act. Now that shows talent and tenacity.

In his later years, he was once asked what he wanted as his epitaph. He paused, thought and answered: "Just two words… I tried."

What a simple statement that speaks volumes. And what great advice as so much of success in business and in life is about trying. You miss all the shots you don't take.

Always remember...ain't no chance unless you take it.

There are the criers, the sighers, the deniers, the highflyers, even the liars. Those who get ahead and stay ahead are the triers.

Harry's Hint

*No one is ever
old enough to
know better.*

10

Many Aspire to Success, but Few Are Willing to Perspire for It

Known as the Dean of Personal Development, Earl Nightingale devoted his life to the study of success. He artfully tells the classic story about a conversation between a farmer and a preacher.

> *The story goes that the preacher was driving down a country road when he came upon the most beautiful farm he'd ever seen in his lifetime spent traveling rural roads. He could only compare it to a beautiful painting. It was by no means a new farm, but the house and buildings were well constructed and in perfect repair and paint. A garden*

around the house was filled with flowers and shrubs. A fine row of trees lined each side of the white gravel drive. The fields were beautifully tilled, and a fine herd of fat dairy cattle grazed knee-deep in the pasture. The site was so arresting that the preacher stopped to drink it all in. He had been raised on a farm himself, and he knew a great one when he saw it.

It was then he noticed the farmer, on a tractor, hard at work, approaching the place where the preacher stood beside his car.

When the farmer got closer, the preacher hailed him. The farmer stopped the tractor, idled down the engine, and then shouted a friendly "hello!"

The preacher said to him, "My good man, God has certainly blessed you with a magnificent farm."

And then, there was a pause as the farmer took off his cap and shifted in the tractor seat to take a look at his pride and joy. He then looked at the preacher and said, "Yes, God has, and we're grateful. But you should have seen this place when He had it all to Himself." [ii]

I certainly do not intend to be irreverent. We should count our many God-given blessings. But we should also never lose sight of the fact that we are all blessed, not necessarily with the same land as the farmer in our story, but with similar opportunity. Our success is a direct reflection of what we do with those opportunities. The pride, the satisfaction and the exhilaration of achievement are worth the cost of commitment and hard work. Just ask any successful person you know.

It is said that Thomas Edison contributed his "genius" to 1 percent inspiration and 99 percent perspiration. That's a statistic for sales success if I've ever heard one. Yes, many aspire to success, but few are willing to perspire for it.

Never itch for anything you aren't willing to scratch for.

11

There Aren't Enough Crutches in the World for All the Lame Excuses

Have you heard the story about the youngster who went away to summer camp? One day he went fishing, but he didn't catch anything. When he got back to his cabin, he sat down and wrote the following note to his grandmother:

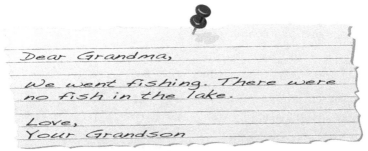

Dear Grandma,

We went fishing. There were no fish in the lake.

Love,
Your Grandson

Cute…and evidence of a positive attitude and healthy self-confidence. He wasn't crushed or even disappointed. It never even occurred to him that he failed to catch a fish. It never entered his mind that his skills might be lacking. But attitude and confidence do not carry the day, nor ensure against negative results. Just because you believe or wish something to be true doesn't always make it so.

Success takes preparation, planning and action.

Our young camper never thought to question the time of day he went fishing or his rod, reel, bait or lures. He just concluded there were no fish in the lake.

Now, the point is, many salespeople are guilty of the same "logic." When they don't achieve the results they want, they place blame where it does not belong. They ignore the fact that they have not prepared themselves, learned enough or stayed at the task long enough. They fail to plan, which in reality means they plan to fail.

Are you like our youngster who, at the end of a bad day, concludes there are no fish in the pond?

When You Get Something for Nothing, You Just Haven't Been Billed Yet

Now there's a truism if ever I've heard one.

The idea that you can get something for nothing is both a fable and a foible.

Speaking of a fable, Richard Scott Brannon penned this story more than 50 years ago. The lesson is just as relevant today as it was then.

> *Once upon a time a long time ago, a king called the wise men of his kingdom together to challenge them to*

compile for him all the wisdom of the ages. They worked diligently for years before returning with their conclusions bound in just 12 volumes.

The king complimented them for their efforts, but insisted that their work was much too long. Challenged, the wise men returned to the task, intent on condensing the material. Many months later they returned…this time with only one volume. Again they were commended by their ruler, but once more were told to make the information even briefer.

Could they possibly condense all the wisdom of the ages into less than one volume? Undaunted, they once again returned to their awesome responsibility. Finally, the kingdom's wisest men brought in their findings…the result of years of research and painstaking deliberation.

They handed the king a small slip of paper. They had incredibly distilled all the wisdom of the ages into one sentence containing just five words. One could feel the king's anticipation as he carefully unfolded the slip of paper. The sentence read: "THERE AIN'T NO FREE LUNCH!" [iii]

Grammar aside, they had done it!

Far too many people never learn the lesson that success is not free. They go through life looking for or expecting a free lunch. Sure, they occasionally "score," but too often these are one-off victories.

Sustained success comes from digging in (and sometimes digging out)...from accepting risk and playing fair...from giving both effort and energy...and from paying your dues and paying the price.

13

You Get More Than You Give, When You Give More Than You Get

There are many lessons to be learned from the pulpit, but here's a story about a preacher who learned a valuable lesson through the wisdom of a child.

A Pennsylvania Dutch minister who had no regular church filled vacant pulpits around the countryside. One Sunday, accompanied by his small son, he boarded a bus and journeyed several miles to a small town where he was to conduct the morning services.

As he entered the church, he noticed a box in the vestibule bearing the sign, "For the Poor." While he himself was not blessed with an abundance of worldly goods, he produced a quarter from his pocket and dropped it in the box.

At the conclusion of the service, one of the officers of the church thanked him for the sermon and stated that it was the custom of the congregation to give their visiting preacher the contents of the "poor box."

When the official unlocked it, out dropped nothing but the minister's own quarter. He pocketed it with a wry smile, and he and his son started back to the bus station. As they walked, the boy looked up at his father and said, "You'd have gotten more out of it if you had put more in it, wouldn't you, Pop?" [iv]

Simple, but profound. And so true about our jobs and our very lives. What we put in is not only repaid, but earns interest. Make your job important, and it will return the favor.

The person who never does any more than he gets paid for, never gets paid for any more than he does.

14

Never Forget That
Your Work Is a Self-Portrait

The *Mishnah* is a collection of Jewish sayings and traditions and is a basic part of the Talmud. Among the countless lessons is one that says each of us has three names:

The one given by our parents,

The one we are called by others, and

The one we earn for ourselves.

You earn your name and your reputation every day by what you do...and what you don't do.

Do you show up on time...in time...every time... enough times? Do you keep your word...all the time...in all circumstances? Do you sell solutions rather than just a product or service? Are you learning enough...caring enough...doing enough to earn the name you want to be called?

Do you act on your own advice? Is your example one to emulate? Nobel Prize-winning philosopher Albert Schweitzer said it best: "Example is not the main thing in influencing others, it's the only thing."

Harry's
Hint

One of life's hardest
lessons is learning which
bridges to cross and
which to burn.

15

Waiting for Your Ship to Come in Is a Good Way to Miss the Boat

In the days before modern harbors, ships had to wait for the incoming tide to make it into port. Captain and crew were ready and well prepared for the moment when they could ride the turn of the tide, for they knew if they missed it, they would have to wait for another tide to come in.

The English word "opportunity" is derived from the Latin term "ob portu," which refers to a ship standing just outside port, waiting for the best combination of wind, current and tide. In his famous work, *Julius Caesar*, William Shakespeare turned the etymology of "opportunity" into one of his most famous passages:

> *"There is a tide in the affairs of men which, taken at the flood, leads on to fortune;*
>
> *Omitted, all the voyage of their life is bound in shallows and in miseries;*
>
> *On such a full sea are we now afloat;*
>
> *And, we must take the current when it serves or lose our ventures."*

What our friend William was saying is that timing is important when it comes to taking advantage of opportunities. It's critical whether you are trying to make port or find success in sales.

Do you have a plan? Are you taking advantage of the limited face-to-face time you have with your prospects and customers? Are you considering new markets?

We all have opportunity. We all have our own "ob portu." What we do with that opportunity is the difference.

Opportunists take NOW for an answer.

16

When You Put a Limit on What You Will Do, You Put a Limit on What You Can Do

I love the story about a book salesman who called on a farmer to try and sell him a book on effective farming.

The farmer asked, "Why do I need it?"

The salesman quickly and confidently replied, "Because it will teach you how to farm better."

The farmer thought for a minute and said, "Young man, I don't farm half as well as I know how to already."

How appropriate…how true…how sad…and how telling.

Very few people do anything to the best of their ability. They often know the way; they just let life's detours get in the way.

Most of us are like 10-speed bikes – we have gears we never use.

Too many salespeople are hurt far more by what they *won't* do than what they *can't* do. Most limitations and barriers are self-imposed. While you can't control everything that happens, you can always control your own actions.

Almost 2,500 years ago, Greek philosopher Aristotle reportedly said, "Whatever lies within our power to do, lies also within our power not to do."

17

Self-Discipline Is the Original Do-It-Yourself Job

Years ago, I read, clipped and filed the best piece I've ever read about self-discipline. It is truly a blueprint for success. Unfortunately, I don't know who wrote it.* I just know I wish I had. Please forgive the gender bias…it is appropriate for everyone.

The longer I live, the more weight I attach to a man's ability to manage and discipline himself. The longer I live, the more firmly convinced I become that the essential factor which lifts a man above his fellows in terms of achievement and success is his superior capacity for self-discipline.

Talent plays its part, of course, but talent or aptitude is not the difference. Every day in every field of endeavor, we see talented men whose special abilities are wasting away, contributing little to the success of the individual or the good of mankind; and every day we observe others who are less gifted but have accomplished more.

Education is a priceless aid to success, of course, but education is not the difference. The educated derelict is a common sight, and so is the man who has achieved resounding success without the opportunity for, or the advantages of, a formal education. We can only conclude that while formal schooling is an important advantage, it is not a guarantor of success nor is its absence a fatal handicap.

There are those who profess to believe that the difference between one man's achievement and another's is largely a matter of luck. Don't you believe it! You and I both know the truth of that classic phrase:"It's a funny thing about luck…the harder I work, the luckier I get."

Is the difference a matter of differing levels of intelligence? I believe not; even though manifestly, the man or woman endowed with a superior intellect, a higher-than-average I.Q., is fortunate on that account and thus possesses a running start toward success, but we have all seen within our own field of observation that the relationship between intelligence and accomplishment is something less than constant.

The conclusion is inescapable that high intelligence doesn't necessarily guarantee success or achievement, and that average mentality can and often does achieve far better than average results.

I'm totally convinced that the essential, fundamental, underlying difference between one man and the next, one of whom becomes a man of accomplishment while the other remains an "excuse maker," is the former's greater capacity to manage himself.

The man with the true capacity for self-discipline can tell himself to get up in the morning and not need someone else to sweep him out of bed. He can tell himself to start a course of study and carry it through and need no policeman to see that he does so. He can tell himself to drink and eat with moderation and make it stick. He can tell himself to do an honest day's work and then do it whether someone watches him or not.

He can tell himself to do the truly important things first, so that if there isn't enough time to go around and something must be neglected, it will be the less essential tasks. He can tell himself to save the first few pennies out of each dollar of income (not pennies "left over") and can resist temptations which would destroy his financial plans and his economic hopes. He can make himself do what he says he will do. He can make himself finish the job he starts, carry out his plans, start in time and be there on time. He can discipline himself so well that no one else needs to do so; and because he can, he is a MAN and not a boy. And because he is a man capable of self-discipline, he surely is, or in course of time, he will surely be, a man of achievement and distinction.

Now here is the most interesting thing about self-discipline: He who wants it may have it…if he wants it **enough**!

If you were born without an ear for music, you can't give yourself that talent by wanting it. If you have no natural athletic ability, you probably can't be better than a passably good athlete no matter how much you want to be a star. Whatever your I.Q. was at age four – so they tell us – it will tend to remain constant all your life no matter what you do about it.

But the capacity for self-discipline, more important than any of these, is something we **can** generate within ourselves! And what a happy and wonderful truth this is – that the one ingredient we most need is ours for the asking, for the wanting…if only we want it **enough**. We need no special talent, no advanced education, no "luck," no *superior intellect, to discipline ourselves more effectively tomorrow than we did today. We need only the resolute determination to do so!*

*All you need to do is this: Beginning this very day, stop doing some **one** thing you know you should not do and start doing each day some **one** thing you know you should do. That's all!*

Then a little later, when you have these two things mastered, try two more…then later two more…and then, still more. Stay with it long enough and the world will be yours!

Everything in life ultimately comes down to self- discipline.

The other "selfs" are critical to quality of life and success: self-esteem, self-awareness, self-reliance and self- confidence. But the most important of all is self-discipline. No excuses, no passing the buck, no finger pointing…it's all up to you.

*I have searched in vain to find the original author of this article. It has been attributed to various people, including Benjamin N. Woodson. If you know who wrote it, please let me know so I can give him/her due credit.

18

Sometimes You Do Have to Sweat the Small Stuff

Little things mean a lot. Small actions…or omissions…can result in large consequences. Consider this proverb, which dates back to the 14th century and has taken on many variations over the centuries:

For want of a nail, the shoe was lost;

For want of a shoe, the horse was lost;

For want of a horse, the rider was lost;

For want of a rider, the message was lost;

For want of the message, the battle was lost;

For want of a battle, the kingdom was lost;

And all for the want of a nail.

A simple lesson but a profound impact. We all are only as strong as our weakest link.

A popular book from recent years proclaimed that we shouldn't sweat the small stuff. There is a great deal of wisdom in the idea of putting what happens to us in life in the proper perspective and not letting the little things drive us crazy.

Yet there is no doubt as to the importance of little things. They do mean a lot! For successful salespeople, the "little things" can include:

- Writing a thank-you note for an order.

- Sending a birthday or anniversary card.

- Forwarding an article about your customer or about a topic useful to them.

- Offering a helpful suggestion that might make a customer's business better.

- Sharing a lead.

- Practicing kindness and caring.

These should be part of your daily thoughts and actions.

Don't you fail...for the want of a nail.

19

Obstacles Are Opportunities in Disguise

Getting your "foot in the door" is a must if you're going to make it in sales. It's an obstacle every salesperson has to overcome. Some prospects make inaccessibility an art form, while others treat salespeople as if they are the exclusive distributors of some communicable disease.

One of the best salespeople I ever knew was a Zep, Inc. pioneer named Sidney Kogan. Of all the "pros" I have been fortunate to work with, he would be the person I would want with me if my very life depended on getting an order. Sid was imaginative and always found a way to get an audience with a prospect. He had enough showmanship to entertain, along with enough sincerity to instill confidence. Of the many stories

I could tell about Sid, here is just one that portrays his ability to see opportunities where others saw obstacles.

One day, Sid was in a small Georgia town training a new salesperson on how to get that first meeting with a prospect. He bet the trainee a lunch that he could open a new account with the town's leading bank. The new salesman was aware that banks were difficult prospects, so the dare was accepted.

Sid straightened his tie, bounded across the street and confidently strode through the bank's front door. He asked to see the manager who was, in fact, the bank's president. When the president appeared, Sid introduced himself and stated that he would like to open an account.

"Fine, Mr. Kogan, do come in," the president said as he ushered Sid into his office.

When the president asked what kind of account he would like to open, savings or checking, Sid replied, "No, sir, you've got it backwards. It's *your* account I would like to open. I want you to open an account with me."

The bank president smiled. He knew he'd been had, but he enjoyed it. Sid got to tell his sales story, and a few minutes later, he had his order, as well as a new friend…not to mention his free lunch.

A great deal of what we see depends on what we are looking for.

A resourceful person sees opportunity when others see only obstacles.

20

You've Gotta Make Mistakes if You're Gonna Make Good Decisions

"Sir, what is the secret of your success?" a reporter asked a company president.

"Two words," the president replied. "Right decisions." "And how do you make the right decisions?"

"One word: *experience.*"

"And how do you get experience?" "Two words: *wrong decisions.*"

It sounds so simple, but we learn from our mistakes. Rarely do we get things exactly right the first time. Learn from your mistakes and don't be paralyzed by them. If at first you don't succeed, you're running about average.

The best attitude to have about selling is a "keep-at-it-tude."

What great advice for a salesperson. Keep experimenting… keep taking risks…keep making mistakes…keep learning… keep on keeping on.

Harry's
Hint

The best way to keep from
being unemployed is to
work at it.

21

Those Who Mind Their Business Usually Have Good Ones

William M. Scholl, a podiatrist, founded Dr. Scholl's in 1906. The good doctor, who was an extremely inventive person, amassed a fortune selling bunion and corn pads, arch preservers and numerous other foot care products. His company gained international fame and at one time was a member of the prestigious Fortune 500.

In the early days of the company, in each of his locations was a sign above every cash register that read: "If it isn't right, it's wrong."

Wow! What a credo...what an effective way to run your business and your life.

We don't have to look far to find examples of "wrong." When was the last time you left a post office happy? When were you last satisfied after trying to speak to a live human at the IRS, a large corporation, your bank or a municipal government office?

More than 100 years ago, Dr. Scholl had it right...if it isn't right, it's wrong. No wavering, no excuses. If you make a mistake and don't correct it, you've made two.

It's really not that hard to do the right thing. Practice the Golden Rule – not some of the time, but all of the time. Former UCLA basketball coach John Wooden said it best: "If you don't have time to do it right, when will you have the time to do it over?"

The time is always right to do what is right.

There is no right way to do the wrong thing. Do right by your customers, and they will do right by you.

22

Selling Is a Trick, but It Isn't Trickery

I have a friend who today is a very successful executive, but still a salesman at heart. His integrity is unquestioned, and he has an extraordinary sense of fair play. If a customer is ever unhappy, he has no time-limit on returns. Credit memos and "your money back" are the principles by which he runs his business. But it wasn't always that way.

As a streetwise, hustling (make that hustler) young man on the "grow," my friend's value system was just forming and still rough around the edges. Among the many ventures he explored was selling prophylactics.

Not having the resources to manufacture condoms, but recognizing the potential, he began a distributorship. Vending was his game, and there was "cash in condoms." His business grew, and soon his 50-cent condom vending machines could be found in men's bathrooms across the country. He prospered, and with his markups, he was truly both a robber and a rubber baron.

Even though his business was going well, Mr. Prophylactic was restless. Good was not good enough, and he sought a way to grow his business. One day it occurred to him that women were the true losers in "accidents," so why not place condom vending machines in ladies' restrooms as well? The idea caught on, and before long his revenues from each location doubled.

The story should end here, but unfortunately it doesn't. My friend would not leave well enough alone and looked for yet another way to improve his profitability.

Times were different back then. Women were less assertive, and sex (for the most part) was still "in the closet." Realizing this, Mr. Prophylactic decided not to fill the machines in the ladies' restrooms with merchandise, but rather to leave them empty. He had concluded that only one woman in 50 might be comfortable enough to approach the service station or restaurant owner and say, "I put 50 cents in your condom machine and nothing came out."

He was right, and his profits increased measurably. Giving customers value for their money, however, is a basic tenet of good salesmanship. As you might surmise, his fortune was short-lived and his vending days numbered.

While we may be amused by this story, it teaches us a valuable lesson about the difference between using a trick and using trickery to increase sales. A trick is a skillful action...a quicker artful way of getting a result. It differs greatly from trickery, which is deceptive, underhanded or misleading.

As salespeople, we have worked hard to attain professional status, but we still have to overcome many prejudices and preconceived notions. There are still the doubting Thomases who are defensive and on guard as soon as someone says he or she is a salesperson. Unfortunately, too many salespeople resort to trickery and deceit, contributing to the bad press we receive.

By all means, use every *trick* in the sales book to improve your results. Be skillful...be creative...be clever...be resourceful... and always take the high road. Trickery will get you nowhere in the long run. It may win the battle, but it will lose the war.

Let your conscience be your guide...not your accomplice.

Harry's Hint

*Easy street
is a blind alley.*

23

Failure Is the Path of Least Persistence

I recently read a piece about sales *resistance*. The premise was that sales resistance is not up (i.e., increasing), rather sales *persistence* is down (that is, decreasing). Which, by now you've probably realized, reminds me of a story.

An enterprising and successful sales manager was concerned that his sales force was writing far too many orders with just one line item. He concluded that they simply were not asking for additional products. Curious if the same problem existed in other industries, he devised a simple experiment to test his premise.

Our sales manager visited one of his city's leading department stores. Once inside, he chose a counter filled with popular low-priced items. He selected one item and paid for it with a $100 bill. Now, a key part of this experiment was that he had decided ahead of time that no matter what else the salesperson suggested he purchase, he would agree. No hesitation…no objection…he would continue to buy whatever additional items were offered until he spent his entire $100. He made his purchase and left, disappointed that the salesperson never suggested another item.

Realizing that one experience doesn't qualify as a valid experiment, he visited three other department stores and numerous specialty shops. The sad fact is that not once did he spend the entire $100. What a terrible example of today's salesmanship.

In sales, we're all taught to ask for the order. But even with this being drummed into us, we don't practice what has been preached.

Too many salespeople quit selling before their customers quit buying.

Are you leaving additional business "on the counter" by simply not asking? How do you know? One way is to end on a "no" rather than a "yes." Be tactful and respectful, but keep asking for additional items or services until you hear, "I'll stop there" or "Remind me next time" or something definitive that lets you know your customer has quit buying.

You can get rich if you'll remember P.O.O.R. – Persistence Often Overcomes Resistance. Make a habit of being persistent. Make good habits, and they will make you.

24

A Problem Well Put Is Half Solved

As a salesperson, you need to understand that a major part of solving a problem is to first *correctly* define it. Don't "tilt at windmills" like Cervantes' fictional character Don Quixote, who misapplied his romantic heroism by attacking imaginary adversaries. Here is an old fable that illustrates how important it is to ask the right questions before trying to solve a problem.

A king had an infestation of mice in his palace. He went to his counselors, who advised him to hire some cats. The cats cleared the palace of the mice, but they multiplied...quickly! The king returned to his wise men, complaining about his cat infestation. This time they counseled him to get some dogs. Well, the dogs soon ousted the cats. They also began sleeping on the king's bed and being a general nuisance by barking at his guests and howling all night long.

Returning again to his counselors, the king was told that lions would scatter the dogs, which, of course, they did. Before long, however, the lions were lounging on the couches and eating the king's store of fine meats.

"What am I to do now?" he quizzed his wise men.

"Get some elephants!" they said.

Sure enough, the elephants drove out the lions, but they played havoc with the palace, crushing furniture and leaving unseemly droppings.

"Now what?" the king asked his advisors.

"Bring in some mice," said the wise men. "They will scare the elephants away!"

Far too often we try to resolve problems with solutions that only lead to other problems. Our king ended up with mice again because his "wise men" never bothered to ask why there were mice in the palace in the first place.

Albert Einstein once said, "If I had an hour to solve a problem, I'd spend 55 minutes thinking about the problem and 5 minutes thinking about solutions."

First define…then analyze…then strategize…and *then* set about solving the problem. Think of consequences as well as solutions.

If you use a "ready-fire-aim" approach to challenges, you'll miss the mark every time.

25

A Friend Is a Gift That You Give Yourself

Many years ago, I attended the University of Florida. It was my first time away from home, and I was homesick. In a moment of loneliness and despair, I sent a telegram (I did say it was many years ago!) to my father that said simply:

Dear Dad,

Am without money or friends.

Love, Harry

My father immediately sent a telegram back that said:

Dear Harry,

Make friends.

Love, Dad

Although my father was not a salesman, he couldn't have offered better sales advice.

I greatly value education, skills, theories and statistical validation. I respect PowerPoint™ presentations, economic justifications and value propositions. But, I've also learned there is a critical human side to sales success that involves emotion, warmth, respect, trust and friendship.

People buy from people they like.

A long-standing business axiom states, "All things being equal, people want to do business with their friends. Even when all things are not equal, people still want to do business with their friends."

Abraham Lincoln once reportedly said, "If you would win a man to your cause, first convince him that you are his sincere friend."

Give yourself a gift…make friends.

26

No One Ever Listened Himself Out of a Sale

I've often shared this story from author Eugene Raudsepp:

A zoologist was walking down a busy city street with a friend. In the midst of the honking horns and screeching tires, he exclaimed to his friend, "Listen to that cricket!"

The friend looked at the zoologist in astonishment and said, "You hear a cricket in the middle of all this noise and confusion?"

Without a word, the zoologist reached into his pocket, took out a coin, and flipped it into the air. As it clinked on the sidewalk, a dozen heads turned in response.

The zoologist said quietly to his friend, "We hear what we listen for." [v]

Our zoologist is a wise man! There is a vast difference between selective listening and active listening. (Most of our spouses accuse us of selective listening, and too often, they're right!)

An old adage points out that many people watch but few really see. It's just as true that many people hear, but few really listen. Perhaps it's human nature to selectively listen. We filter what we hear through our interests, desires, past experiences and preconceived notions. We listen to what we want to hear… and tune out what we don't want to hear.

Top salespeople keep an eye and an ear out for opportunity. We often think of salespeople glibly talking themselves into sales, but the best salespeople actively listen themselves into even more orders and success.

The 80/20 rule in business also holds true for selling – a good salesperson should listen 80 percent of the time and talk 20 percent. You often hear, "He talks too much," but when did you last hear, "He listens too much"? Good listeners are not only popular, after a while they actually know something.

One of the best ways to persuade others is with your ears.

Give your full attention to customers rather than thinking about what you're going to say next. Don't let your "filters" diminish, or worse yet, eliminate the signs and signals that translate into sales. Focus not only on what is said, but what isn't said by "listening between the lines" to understand what is meant.

"It's just not cricket" to not use all your senses. We are blessed with two ears and one mouth. There's a lesson in that physiology…your ears can out-earn your mouth.

27

The Safest Gamble of All Is to Take a Chance on Yourself

I remember many years ago calling on an antiques dealer to sell him brass polish and other refurbishing materials. His father, who was retired, always spent his afternoons piddling around the son's showroom. During the course of my regular visits, the old gentleman and I became friends.

One day as we were talking, I asked him, "Pop, why did you immigrate to America?"

In his heavy Greek accent, he told me a story that serves as a lesson for us all:

I was just a young boy in Greece, but I knew my opportunities were limited. I had seen my parents' and relatives' health hurt by the harsh conditions we lived in. Every night, I dreamed about America and read everything I could get my hands on about this great country. Finally, I got up enough courage to go talk with my father.

"Papa," I said, "I want to go to America."

My father pushed his cap to the back of his head, smiled and said, "My son, America is a big country, a tough and demanding country. It needs men...strong men. What can a small boy like you do?"

I looked back at my father and said, "Papa, I can grow."

And grow he did. While never big in stature, my friend grew in heart, in spirit and in boundless optimism. His story is truly the story of America. What a wonderful legacy my old friend gave us.

Success does not demand that we be perfect. It requires only that we grow. To be an effective salesperson, you must be more tomorrow than you are today.

To better yourself, first make yourself better.

28

You Never Get Rewarded for the Things You Intend to Do

I love the lesson to be learned from a simple math problem:

Three frogs sat on a log. One decided to jump off. How many frogs were left on the log?

BevsArt.com

Answer: Three.

Almost everyone answers "two." Just because one frog *decided* to jump off does not mean it actually did.

So often there are gaps between what we decide to do and what we actually do. We *decide* to lose weight, exercise or quit smoking. We *decide* to set goals, make more calls or work harder. But for whatever reason or excuse, we just don't follow through. As the old proverb says, "The road to hell is paved with good intentions."

Action trumps inaction. Right now is a good time to take action.

Winning starts with beginning.

The best-laid plans of mice and men don't mean a thing until you begin.

Harry's Hint

The road to success is always under construction.

29

The Surest Way to Mishandle a Problem Is to Avoid Facing Up to It

I have a good friend who is a successful doctor. He once told me of an incident that occurred when he was a young intern at a hospital in Atlanta, Georgia.

After the death of the first patient who passed away under his care, he was charged with sharing the sad news with the family. He was nervous, uncertain and wary of speaking to the loved ones who gathered around him. Of course, he wanted to be gentle and thoughtful.

My friend began by explaining that the patient's respiration was shallow and slow. "His blood pressure dropped and was unobtainable, and there was no longer a pulse," he continued. "His heartbeat ultimately ceased."

At the time, it was the hospital's policy to get the family to sign an autopsy request. They did, and he thanked them.

As he was turning to leave, one of the family members asked, "Doc, do you think he's going to make it through the night?"

He quickly learned a powerful lesson: Be kind but be direct.

Whether you are in medicine or sales or any other profession, tell it like it is. Say what you mean and mean what you say. Make certain you are understood. Always be honest. If you don't have the answer to a question, say so. Then either try to find the answer or suggest alternatives.

The best way out of difficulty is through it.

30

Don't Bait Your Hook Until You Know What the Fish Will Bite

In his book, *How to Win Friends and Influence People*, Dale Carnegie relayed a story about American essayist and philosopher Ralph Waldo Emerson and how he and his son failed to do a simple thing for a very simple reason.

One day, a young calf on the Emerson farm broke loose from the barn and wandered away. Emerson caught the calf, and with his son's help, tried to lead the animal back to the barn. First, they coaxed; then they commanded. Next the father and son pushed and pulled. But the calf stubbornly resisted their efforts.

Eventually, the housemaid noticed what they were attempting to do. She had never written an essay or given a philosophical treatise, but she got that calf back into the barn with no trouble whatsoever. She merely put her finger in the calf's mouth and let the animal suckle on it while she gently led it into the barn.

Why did the housemaid succeed while Emerson and his son failed? Carnegie, a human relations expert, pointed out that Emerson and his son were too concerned with what *they* wanted – that is, to get the calf into the barn. The housemaid thought of what the *calf* wanted rather than what *she* wanted.

This little calf story certainly applies to selling. Naturally, *you* want your customer to buy. Does the customer care about your reasons for wanting to complete a sale? Of course not. That's why the most successful selling techniques focus on what the customer wants.

Any good fisherman will tell you that you can't bait your hook until you know what the fish will bite. Questioning, directed toward uncovering your customer's desire, is the approach most likely to lead to a sale.

Always remember: It's not just about you.

Dale Carnegie put it this way: "I am very fond of strawberries and cream. But I find that, for some strange reason, fish prefer worms. So when I go fishing, I don't bait the hook with strawberries and cream."

Nothing is more important than empathy – putting yourself in your customers' shoes...thinking of their problems, in their terms and for their benefit.

31

Choice, Not Chance, Determines Destiny

Robert Schuller was a noted pastor and motivational speaker. He once suggested that people fall into one of four distinct groups:

"First, there are the cop-outs. These people set no goals and make no decisions.

"Second, there are the holdouts. They have a beautiful dream, but they're afraid to respond to its challenge because they aren't sure they can make it. These people have lost all childlike faith.

"Third, there are the dropouts. They start to make their dream come true. They know their role. They set their goals, but when the going gets tough, they quit. They don't pay the toll.

"Finally, there are the all-outs. They are the people who know their role. They want and need and [know they] are going to be stars. ... They want to *shine out* as an inspiration to others.

They set their goals. The all-outs never quit. Even when the toll gets heavy, they're dedicated. They're committed."

Cop-out…holdout…dropout…ALL-OUT – the choice is yours.

You are where you are today because you've chosen to be there.

Harry's Hint

Where it's at
keeps changing.

32

Always Know What You're Talking About, but Don't Always Talk About What You Know

A family with a second grader moved into a new neighborhood. When the young girl returned home from her first day at her new school, she asked her mother, "What's sex?"

Her mother, like most mothers, had been expecting that question for some time and spent the next half hour explaining all about the birds and bees.

With the explanation finished, she asked her daughter, "Now, do you understand all the things I've told you?"

"Yes," her daughter said, "I think I do." She then pulled out the registration form she had brought home to complete so she could get a school library card. Pointing to the section that asked to check a box for sex she asked, "But how am I going to fit all of that into this little square?"

Oops!

This mother reminds me of salespeople who give long, detailed answers before they know the real questions. When a customer asks a question, first be sure you understand it. Then, and only then, answer with just enough information to satisfy and please. You don't have to prove how smart you are. Which brings me to another point....

Many salespeople insist on telling everything they know, and in turn, overstay their welcome and limit their effectiveness. They want to spend their time being educators, and while that's a noble profession, it doesn't always get the order. Remember the old public speaker's principle: "The mind can absorb only what the seat can endure."

You can't know too much, but you can say too much.

How long you talk and how much information you share is an art you must master. A pool hustler once told me he never shows his total game – he just plays well enough to win. The same concept holds true in sales. You should tell just enough to create interest, identify needs, be convincing, answer any questions and, of course, get the order!

33

Don't Wait Until You're in Trouble to Get Moving

Famed and often-quoted storyteller Abraham Lincoln is said to have told a story about a frog that fell into a deep, muddy wagon track. Try as he did to get out, several days later he was still stuck there.

His frog friends found him and urged him to get out of his predicament. He made a few more feeble efforts, but remained mired in his rut. His friends encouraged him to try harder, but they finally gave up and went back to their pond.

The next day, the friends found the frog sunning himself contentedly along the shore of the pond. "How did you get out of that rut?" they asked.

"Well, as you know, I couldn't," said the frog. "But then a wagon came along and I had to." [vii]

We all know what we should do and often what we could do. But too often we don't do it until circumstances require us to do what we must do.

Most of us don't put our best foot forward until we get the other one in hot water.

Don't wait for the wagon to come...provide your own discipline and impetus for success.

34

Salesmanship Is the Art of Letting Someone Else Have Your Way

I've heard salesmanship defined as thinking on your feet. That's not the total answer, but adaptability is an integral part of a superstar salesperson's "adeptability."

Always remember: Different strokes for different folks.

Make sure that whether you're in Rome, New York…Rome, Georgia…or Rome, Italy…you do as those particular Romans do and tailor your message accordingly.

Tailoring your "tale" reminds me of the story of a young, cold-calling insurance salesman. Mustering all his charm, the salesman walked into a business and asked the receptionist if he could see the company's sales manager. She liked his smile and ushered him into the executive's office. After introducing himself, he began with that infamous line, "I don't suppose you want to buy anything, do you?"

"No," replied the sales manager curtly.

"I didn't think so," said the salesman dejectedly as he got up to leave.

"Wait a minute," said the sales manager, "I want to talk with you."

The salesman sat down again, obviously nervous and confused.

"I train salespeople," said the sales manager, "and you're the worst I've ever seen. You'll never sell anything until you display confidence and learn to accentuate the positive. Now, because you're no doubt new at this, I'm going to help you out by signing up for a $10,000 policy."

After the sales manager had signed on the proverbial dotted line, he said, again trying to help, "Young man, one thing you'll have to do is develop a few standard organized sales talks."

"Oh, but I have," replied the salesman smiling. "This is my standard organized sales talk for sales managers."

Adapting to the circumstances can often turn many a harsh "no" into a sweet "yes."

The Best Place to Find a Helping Hand Is at the End of Your Own Arm

Ten is a special number.

The Ten Commandments...the Bill of Rights (the first 10 amendments to the United States Constitution)...a beautiful girl who is called a "10"...the popular "top 10 list."

My favorite "10," when it comes to success, is a simple sentence of just 10 words, each only two letters: *If it is to be, it is up to me*.

It's simple but profound. While there is no "I" in team, there is a "U" in success.

Teamwork, relationships and cooperation are all important. But success starts with you – your initiative, your drive, your determination, your attitude, your resilience. Success is not an individual sport, but it depends on individuals each doing his or her part (and then some).

The best rules of success won't work unless you do.

More often than not, you control your destiny. How else would you want it?

Harry's Hint

The road to success
is dotted with many
tempting parking places.

36

Luck Is Always Against Those Who Depend on It

There's no doubt in my mind of the relationship between luck and hard work…they are inseparable partners.

Years ago I found and clipped some sage advice from a wise man about luck that has stuck with me. I've taken the liberty of updating the language to reflect today's culture and adding a few of my own thoughts, but the core message remains the same:

Do I believe in luck? You bet! It's a wonderful force. I'm familiar with the success stories of too many lucky men and women to doubt its existence and effectiveness.

I've seen some people reach out and grab an opportunity, while others stood around not realizing it was even there. And once having grabbed that opportunity, they hold on with a grip that makes the jaws of a junkyard dog seem like a butterfly's touch.

They have the vision to see the possibilities within each situation, the ambition to desire them and the courage to tackle them.

They intensify their strong points, bolster their weak ones and cultivate those personal qualities that lead others to trust them.

They sow the seeds of sunshine, good cheer, optimism and kindness. They give freely of what they have, both spiritually and physically.

They think a little straighter and work a little harder and a lot longer. They run on nerve and enthusiasm. They always give their best effort.

They keep their heads cool, their feet warm, their minds busy. They don't worry over trivialities. They set a plan and then stick to it, rain or shine.

They talk and act like winners, for they know in time they will be. And, then, as you might imagine…luck does all the rest. [viii]

Luck favors the backbone, not the wishbone.

37

If You Must Speak Your Mind, Mind How You Speak

One day several years ago, my wife and I were taking a car ride with our 5-year-old grandson, Josh, who was in the back seat eating an apple. About halfway through his snack, he asked, "Pop, why is my apple turning brown?"

I explained, "Well, after you bite into the apple, oxygen is introduced and enzymes like polyphenol oxidase react to form compounds that create a sort of rust on the surface, making it appear brown."

After a long pause, Josh said, "Pop, are you talking to me?"

Suddenly I thought of that great line from the movie *Cool Hand Luke*: "What we've got here is a failure to communicate." Josh taught me a lesson that day!

How many times do we as salespeople do the same thing – use jargon, technical terms or otherwise talk over our customers' heads? Your customers must understand what you are saying and what you mean.

People only hear what they understand.

Words are critical, so use them wisely…

- Don't say "covenant" when you mean "guarantee."
- Don't say "perilous" when you mean "dangerous."
- Don't say "innocuous" when you mean "harmless."
- Don't say "demurral" when you mean "disagreement."
- Don't say "price" when you mean "value."

Remember the old acronym K.I.S.S. – Keep It Simple, Stupid.

A story in the Bible states that Samson slew a thousand Philistines with the jawbone of an ass. Twice that many sales are killed every day with the same implement.

Make sure the failure to communicate isn't yours.

38

Ingenuity Is the Key That Opens the Door to Opportunity

Good salespeople know that taking advantage of opportunity often requires imagination and ingenuity. Certainly showing up and having a firm handshake, a cheerful smile, product knowledge and a dozen other ingredients are important. But sometimes it just boils down to creativity. Matching wits, if you will. Getting an edge.

I've known many truly super salespeople throughout my career. What separated them from the pack? What made them so special? They all differed in background, in appearance and in ability. The distinguishing characteristic they all shared was creativity.

Let me give you an example of the type of creativity and imagination I'm talking about, because you won't learn this in any sales training course.

Many years ago, I serviced a particularly good automotive account. Quite naturally, I bought a car from that dealership. (On second thought, maybe it's not so natural, although it should be. It's good business to do business with people who do business with you.)

The salesman with whom I traded was about 75. He had the distinction of being one of the original members of the Ford 500 Club. We became friends, and on one occasion, he told me about a tactic he had used for years whenever customers came in to shop his price or get a quote on a car. If he determined he indeed had a "live one," he would give the prospect all the information and do his best to close the deal.

If the prospect was still reluctant to commit, before letting them leave, my friend would say, "Look, for being so nice and coming in, I have a little something for you."

From a little freezer he kept in his office, he would then pull out a pint of ice cream and give it to the prospective customer.

Now why would my friend do that?

Well, the customer wouldn't want their ice cream to melt, so what would they do? Go straight home to put their gift in the freezer. Which means they *didn't* do what? Go down the street to another dealership to shop the price my friend had quoted or to look for a competing make of automobile. My friend closed many a sale the same evening by a phone call or a visit to the prospect's home.

Brilliant!

Ingenuity and imagination are the allies of every successful salesperson.

39

Fight Truth Decay

Few Americans are quoted more than Abraham Lincoln. More than 150 years ago, he shared thoughts that have become some of our most repeated lines.

One of my favorite quotes is often attributed to Lincoln, although there is healthy debate about whether or not he actually said it: "It is true that you may fool all of the people some of the time; you can even fool some of the people all of the time; but, you can't fool all of the people all of the time."

What is not nearly as well-known is the sentence that preceded his famous quote: "If you once forfeit the confidence of your fellow citizens, you can never regain their respect and esteem."

What a sales manager Honest Abe would have been, as he was talking about simple honesty. Successful salespeople are not honest some of the time. They are truthful and straightforward all of the time. They don't bend the truth to fit the conditions of the moment. They remember, as an earlier chapter stated, that selling is a trick but it isn't trickery.

Nothing undermines customers' confidence faster than twisting the truth. Samuel Langhorne Clemens, better known as American humorist and literary icon Mark Twain, perhaps said it best: "When in doubt, tell the truth."

Honesty isn't just the best policy, it's the only policy.

The Best Time to Plan for Your Future Is Between Yesterday and Tomorrow

A Chinese proverb says, "The best time to plant a tree is 20 years ago. The next best time is today."

The profoundness of this simple statement is remarkable.

Certainly, the best time to do anything for which you could derive benefit was "yesterday." But if by chance you didn't do that, there's no time like the present!

Have the foresight to start planting trees that you will need at some point in your future. Today is the day. Remember…it wasn't raining when Noah built the ark.

Always be on the lookout for "bad weather" and "bumps in the road". Expect the unexpected. Anticipate…observe… prepare and execute.

So, starting today, do and be your best.

It's never too late to be what you might have been.

Harry's Hint

If at first you succeed...
try something harder.

41

A Story a Day Keeps Failure Away

One of the best salespeople I ever knew once asked if I had read *Aesop's Fables*. He thought Aesop was one of the world's best salesmen. I dug out a tattered copy that I had read many times to my children and grandchildren and thumbed through it, recalling some of his explanations.

Take the story of "The Bundle of Sticks" about a farmer who teaches his sons that an individual stick can easily be broken, but a bundle of sticks tied together is strong. What does that have to do with selling? When you're in sales, you're never really on your own. If you were, you too, could be broken. Fortunately, you are "tied" to a strong company, good technical support and customer service, solid training and many sales peers to share with and learn from. Together, you are strong.

In "The Fox and the Grapes," a fox yearns to eat some sweet grapes from a high vine that he can't reach. By convincing himself that he doesn't want the grapes because they are sour, the fox avoids disappointment...but he also doesn't get any grapes! Selling is not a win-all-the-time profession. You're not going to close every sale. The trick is to keep trying, because the sweetness of the wins will long outlast the bitterness of the disappointments.

Don't forget one of my favorites, "The Cat and the Mice." In this story, the mice decide they should tie a bell around the cat to warn them when he is coming. But no mouse is willing to do the job of tying the bell on the cat. The sales lesson? It's easy to make plans, but not so easy to carry them out. Make sure your plans are logical and reasonable and then have the courage to see them through.

Most of us are familiar with "The Ant and the Grasshopper." You may recall that the grasshopper sang all summer while the ant worked hard to store grain. When winter came, the grasshopper – after trying to mooch a few meals from the ant – went hungry and died. Of course it's important to enjoy the moment...to kick back, relax and take it easy once in a while. But don't let that be your modus operandi. The hardest way to do any job is to put it off. Keep an eye on the future…winter is coming.

Lastly, there's the story of "The Dog and the Bone." A dog is carrying a bone when he sees his reflection in the water. Thinking his bone doesn't look very big and perhaps he should find a bigger one, he opens his mouth, and the bone is lost in the water. The moral, of course, is not to be greedy. You should want bigger challenges…better opportunities…larger accounts, but not at the expense of what you have.

There is wisdom (yes, sales wisdom) all around us…in literature…in nature…in everyday life.

Aesop saw it and so did my salesman friend. You can see it too…*if* you look for it.

42

If You Want to Be Original, You Have to Be Yourself

I have always loved the story about a local fisherman and a businessman on vacation from America. It has been told and retold many times in many different places. You may have heard it before, but it is worth repeating.

The tourist complimented the fisherman on the quality of his fish and asked, "How long did it take you to catch these fine fish?"

"Only a little while," the fisherman replied.

The tourist was perplexed. "Then why didn't you stay out longer and catch more?"

"I have enough to support my family and give a few to friends."

The tourist was still confused. "But what do you do with the rest of your time?"

The fisherman smiled and said, "I sleep late, fish a little, play with my children and take a siesta. In the evenings, I go into the village to see my friends. I play the guitar and sing a few songs. As you can see, I have a full life."

The tourist interrupted, "I have an MBA from Harvard; I can help you. You should start by fishing longer every day. You can then sell the extra fish you catch. With the extra revenue, you can buy a bigger boat. With the extra money the larger boat will bring, you can buy a second one, and a third one, and so on, until you have an entire fleet of trawlers. Then, instead of selling your fish to a middleman, you can negotiate directly with a processing plant and maybe even open your own plant. You can leave this little village and move to a big city, maybe Los Angeles or even New York. From there you can direct your huge enterprise...."

The fisherman listened intently, giving the tourist his undivided attention. By the time the "pitch" was done, the fisherman had a few questions.

"How long would that take?"

"Well, to build such an enterprise might take 20 to 25 years," replied the tourist.

"And after that?"

"That's when it gets really interesting," said the businessman. "When your business gets real big, you can start selling stock and make millions."

"Millions?"the fisherman responded. "Really? And after that?" "Well, after that you can retire, live in a tiny village by the sea, sleep late, fish a little, spend time with your children and grandchildren, take a siesta and spend evenings enjoying your friends."

There are many lessons to be learned from this story. One is that while ambition has its place, having the biggest car or the largest house on the hill doesn't guarantee happiness or satisfaction. Learn to be content with where you are. Often what we desire and wish for is exactly what we already have.

Remember...happiness is an inside job.

This story is also a great reminder that you gotta be you. One size does not fit all. Don't let others determine who you are and how you define success. Of course, seek growth and improvement, but always be true to yourself and "do success" your way.

Harry's Hint

The average man has
five senses: touch, taste,
sight, smell and hearing.

The successful man
has two more:
horse and common.

43

The Password to Success Is "NOW"

As the son of a Russian immigrant, I've always loved stories of my ancestors' beginnings and of immigrants establishing themselves in our great country. Here's one you may not have heard about a young man who was somewhat indecisive as to whether or not he should leave his homeland for a new life in America.

For months, the young man received letter after letter from his relatives and friends telling of their new-found prosperity in America. They pleaded with him to join them in the land of opportunity. Every one of them praised their new country and glowingly portrayed its bountiful rewards. They painted pictures of wealth and luxury where, as the stories said, the streets were paved with gold.

Finally, unable to resist the tantalizing temptation, the young man scrimped and saved until he had enough money to come to America and begin his new life. He dreamed of finding the riches he had heard so much about.

After a long voyage across the ocean, he arrived in his new homeland. As he took his first step on American soil, his arms full of packages for his relatives, he looked down. There, at his feet, was a dollar bill. The money reminded him about the opportunity and prosperity that was soon to be his. He thought for a moment about bending down to pick it up. But then, considering his heavy packages, he said, "Oh well, I'll start tomorrow."

The greatest labor-saving device for many people is tomorrow. For procrastinators, the favorite day of the week is someday. "One of these days" becomes none of these days.

Think in terms of today rather than someday. Today demands our attention and commitment.

Successful salespeople know tomorrow never comes. Tomorrow is always the future. And when it arrives, we call it "today" not "tomorrow."

Nike said it best: "Just do it.

But don't just do it...do it NOW!

44

Winning Is a Habit...
Unfortunately, so Is Losing

Here is one of my favorite riddles:

I am your constant companion.

I am your greatest helper or heaviest burden.

I will push you onward or drag you down to failure. I am completely at your command.

Half the things you do might just as well be turned over to me and I will be able to do them quickly and correctly.

I am easily managed – you must merely be firm with me.

Show me exactly how you want something done and after a few lessons, I will do it automatically.

I am the servant of all great people, and alas, of all failures, as well.

Those who are great, I have made great. Those who are failures, I have made failures.

I am not a machine, though I work with all the precision of a machine plus the intelligence of a person.

You may run me for profit or run me for ruin – it makes no difference to me.

Take me, train me, be firm with me, and I will place the world at your feet.

Be easy with me and I will destroy you. Who am I?

I am habit! [ix]

– Anonymous

We are the end product of our habits. Top golfers will tell you "muscle memory" is key to success. Top sales performers will tell you the same key is found in good habits. In fact, good habits and a positive attitude often have a greater impact on achieving success than talent.

Warren Buffett said, "Good habits once established are just as hard to break as bad habits." Wise words from the "Oracle of Omaha."

So what are some of the good habits that sales pros must develop? My list includes preparation, integrity, punctuality, enthusiasm, study, curiosity, routine, consistency, discipline, proper rest, good nutrition and regular exercise, to name just a few. Form them…practice them…repeat them until they become ingrained and involuntary.

Habits are first cobwebs, then cables.

Habits start off frail but, with practice, grow ever stronger until they become nearly impossible to break. Make certain your habits support your success.

45

The Thing to Try
When All Else Fails Is... Again

I've always heard that if a cat sits on a hot stove, it will never again sit on a hot stove. No surprise there...pretty smart cat.

But I've also heard that cat will never again sit on a cold stove, either. Hmmm...maybe that cat isn't so smart after all.

There is an important sales lesson there: Beware of "hot stoves," but don't avoid "all stoves."

In other words, don't let failure go to your head. Don't let the first "no" deter you from going back again.

Success is not permanent; the same is also true of failure.

One failure isn't fatal. Analyze your missteps…then be smart enough not to make the same mistakes again. Take calculated risks for appropriate rewards.

And remember – the only time you don't want to fail is the last time you try.

Harry's Hint

The extra mile has no
traffic jams.

46

Knowing Your Weaknesses Is as Important as Knowing Your Strengths

You may be familiar with one of the heroes of Greek mythology: Achilles. So the story goes, Achilles' mother dipped him into the River Styx to make him invulnerable in battle. When she did, she held him by his heel. As it was untouched by the magic water, it became his only vulnerable spot.

Achilles was a great warrior. But his enemy, Paris, knew his history and shot him in the heel with an arrow, which ultimately caused his death. To this day, the term "Achilles heel" means a person's point of weakness.

Psychologically, we all have an Achilles heel. Our fears and vulnerabilities range far and wide. They can include an inability to take criticism, fear of rejection, fear of failure, refusal to face reality or reluctance to accept responsibility. These weaknesses can stunt our development as salespeople.

Professional vulnerabilities can be as simple as being unprepared for a sales call, cutting corners, bending the truth, not knowing your products/services well enough or speaking badly of the competition...all things that could ultimately bite you "you know where."

Never ignore your weaknesses.

Knowing your weaknesses is the first step in overcoming their consequences. The second step is to find a way to strengthen those weaknesses or compensate for them. After all, if Achilles had worn boots, the story would have likely ended differently.

47

The Best Way to Get "Ahead" Is to Use Yours

When my oldest grandchild, Josh, was about 12 years old, he began spending time at our family's car dealership. He was fascinated with the car business and anxious to learn as much as he could about it. One day when we were having one of our grown-up chats, he asked, "Pop, how do you sell a car?"

In turn, I asked him, "Josh, how would *you* sell a car?"

"Well, I'd go up to the person when he came in and ask him if I could show him a car."

"That's right," I said. "And what would you do then?"

"I'd show him a car, and if he liked it, I'd ask him if he would like to drive it."

"Josh, that's great. What would you do when he got back from the test drive?"

"I'd tell him how much it cost and ask him if he wanted to buy it," Josh answered.

At this point, I was thinking the boy was destined for sales success. But I kept digging. "That's terrific. But what if he said that the car was too much money?"

He thought for a minute and said, "Then I'd show him another car that cost less."

Now I was really impressed. "Okay, what would you do if the customer said he wanted the nicer car but at the lower price of the second car?"

Josh thought for quite a bit. Finally he looked up and said, "Pop, that's too hard for me."

Wouldn't it be nice if we could just say, "That's too hard for me," when confronted with hard questions, tough problems or difficult choices? As salespeople (and adults), that's not an option.

When you are in front of a prospect or customer, you must be ready to answer difficult questions, resolve disputes and sometimes help them make tough decisions. That comes from anticipating the questions, expecting the unexpected, thinking on your feet, adapting, and seeing the future before it arrives. If you can do that, nothing will be too hard for you.

Yes, using your head is definitely the way to get ahead.

The good Lord gave us two ends – one for thinking and one for sitting. Success depends upon which one we use. Heads we win, tails we lose.

48

The Hardest Thing to Get Is Going

Too often it seems that we are intent on making business complicated. Certainly there is a time and place for strategic plans, analyses, matrices and interpolations. But underlying all the sophistication is a simple, undeniable truth, beautifully told through this story:

Once upon a time long ago, there was an old man with a rowboat who ferried passengers across a mile-wide river for 10 cents.

One day a passenger asked, "How many times a day do you do this?"

The old man said, "As many times as I can, because the more I go, the more I get. And, if I don't go…I don't get." [x]

What advice…what a game plan…what a template for success!

As simple as it seems, when you think about it, all you need to know about prosperity and success is "the more you go, the more you get."

Too many people quit looking for work when they find a job.

As the old colloquial saying goes, "There ain't hardly no business 'round here that ain't been went out after."

49

Chance Always Favors the Prepared

Years ago, a movie studio advertised in several New York newspapers to fill a vacancy on its sales force. One applicant replied:

Dear Sir,

I am presently selling furniture at the address below. You may judge my ability as a salesman if you will stop in to see me at any time, pretending that you are interested in buying furniture. When you come in, you may identify me by my red hair, and I will have no way of identifying you. The professional salesmanship I exhibit during your visit will be no more than my usual and effective work-a-day approach to my responsibilities and not an effort to impress a prospective employer.

From more than 1,500 applicants, the redhead got the job. [xi]

Our industrious salesperson was confident enough to take the test, and he passed. Would you be willing to do the same?

Top salespeople only have "on"switches.

They are at the top of their game all the time.

Are you always "on"…always prepared…always doing your best?

I hope so, for every day you are being evaluated, judged and tested. You never know who is watching and considering you for the next job, opportunity or promotion.

50

It's Not Just Who You Know, It's Who Knows You

There are many factors that go into becoming a successful salesperson…integrity, knowing your "stuff," work ethic, resilience and enthusiasm, to name just a few. One that is often overlooked is having a memorable personal brand.

For the many years I was at Zep, we were generous users of advertising specialties. A "Zep Rep" rarely made a sales call without leaving behind a pen, bookmark, screwdriver, keychain or some other Zep-emblazoned novelty. I always carried pen lights imprinted with the Zep logo and tagline, "First in Maintenance…Clean Across America."

Over the years, I gave away literally thousands of pen lights to prospects, customers, friends and many a stranger. They were low cost, but so useful and well appreciated. And…they were disposable. When the batteries died, guess who got a phone call? You guessed it – Harry. Of course, I was always more than happy to comply with a replacement.

You would be amazed at the doors those Zep pen lights opened for me…and kept open. My little flashlights helped me build my brand. So many times I heard: "Hi, Harry, good to see you. Where's my flashlight?"

There are few things more important in sales than creating a memorable, personal brand – something about you that sets you apart from the crowd. Because when it comes to sales, it's not just who you know, but who knows you.

There are lots of ways to become known. You can become an expert on a particular subject and teach or write about that topic. Get involved in community affairs – coach a youth group or volunteer at your church, synagogue or children's school. Separate yourself from the pack by telling jokes, dressing uniquely or adopting a nickname or clever catchphrase.

You can leave behind a flower, candy or note card with a helpful hint. Your "calling card" doesn't have to be expensive, just different. Remember the old salesman's adage: If you make sales calls empty handed, you'll come out the same way.

There are hundreds of ways to build a memorable brand. Find your own way to differentiate yourself, whether it be an advertising specialty, icebreaker or other friend-maker.

Give people a reason to remember you.

When I retired from Zep, my children said to me, "Pop, we hope you can live without the job. We really hope you can live without the money. But we know you can't live without the flashlights."

They gave me customized pen lights with "Harry" rather than "Zep" in the familiar oval logo. While they never admitted who was the culprit, they altered the tagline to read, "First in HIGH Maintenance." They know their dad.

They also know that I love novelties and that I'm a leave-behind kind of guy. Now, anyone who spends time with me gets a Harry's pen light. Come see me in Atlanta, and I'll give you one. Then you, too, will become part of my "family."

The Best Salespeople
Know How to Take a Hint

More than 30 years ago, Robert Fulghum wrote a bestseller entitled *All I Really Need to Know I Learned in Kindergarten*. I highly recommend you read it if you haven't or reread it if it's been a few years. Some of the profound things he said he learned early on about life could also apply to sales:

- Play fair;

- Clean up your own mess;

- Say you're sorry when you hurt someone;

- Live a balanced life;

- Don't take things that aren't yours;

- Put things back where you found them; and

- Flush.

I feel a certain kinship with Robert Fulghum because all I really need to know I learned from more than 50 years in sales. Fifty years of listening and questioning and reading and learning. Fifty years of observing the best. Fifty years of jotting down good ideas and snippets of wisdom. Here is my list of Harry's Most Helpful Hints:

- "I will" is more important than I.Q.

- A great deal of what we see depends on what we're looking for.

- Don't cut what you can untie.

- High touch trumps hi-tech.

- You can get everything you want in life if you help enough people get what they want.

- Nothing happens until somebody sells something.

- The only thing more painful than learning from experience is not learning from experience.

- There is no finish line.

- Never say die until you've done it.

- Know that there are no shortcuts to success.

- The easiest way to get ahead isn't very.

There you have it. Years and years of telling and selling…winning and losing…distilled into a helpful handful of bullet points. Let me end with this one final hint:

Part of knowing what you want is knowing what you would give up to get it.

So, pay the price–in self-discipline…in passionate application of your skills – and success will be yours.

Harry's Hint

Life is like a buffet line.
There aren't any waiters,
so you have to help yourself.

ACKNOWLEDGMENTS

It would be hard to begin my acknowledgments without one last, brief story:

It has long been said that anytime you see a turtle on top of a fence post, you know it had some help getting there.

It seems I'm a bit like a turtle on a fence post. Any success I've enjoyed took lots of help from lots of people. Let me thank so many of you who had more impact and influence on me than you might have imagined.

Thanks to my first, my only and my "trophy" wife, Sherry, who has always been there for me with love and support. What a jewel.

I was blessed with parents and equally blessed with children and grandchildren who make "Pop" feel very special. You "guys" are great!

What a wonderful mentor, boss and friend I had for more than 50 years in Erwin Zaban. His influence and example made so many people better than they thought they could be. I'm living proof.

I used to joke with my business associates that I couldn't have done it without them...or people very much like them. What a fib! I was always protected, supported, encouraged and made to look good because of their efforts, loyalty and dedication. Thank you...Sid Kirschner, John Harper, Allen Soden, Glen Reed, the Docs (Friedman, Fineman and Weller), Garland Monroe, Richard Manning, Logan Harrison, Forrest Neese, George Arkedis, Dan Padgett, Angie Carr, and the many others across Zepland and throughout the world.

Thanks also to Dr. Tim Mescon, Dr. Craig Aronoff, Dr. Gary Selden, Dr. Terry Loe, Dr. Fred Broder, Dr. David Shepherd, Chick Waddell, Jeffrey Gitomer, Jack Halpern, Lee Katz, Mike Wien, Leo Benatar, Perry (Pete) Morris, and Donna Fleishman, who not only encouraged me, but helped me to understand the pitfalls and process of getting a book finished. And a special thank you to Ed Baker, former publisher of the *Atlanta Business Chronicle* and current Executive in Residence at Georgia State

University, for his urging and support. You all were incredibly helpful.

And, of course, thank you to Melissa Farr for her creative design work and to Juli Baldwin and The Baldwin Group for their professionalism, hand-holding, tough questions and editorial services.

Finally, I know I've missed many friends and associates who should be mentioned. I apologize. Please forgive me and know I'm eternally appreciative. We are all products of our experiences and relationships. I treasure mine and continue to benefit from my relationships with all of you.

Again, my sincere thanks. And to all…good health, good times and good selling.

ABOUT THE AUTHOR

Harry Maziar has always been a salesman. From a front-yard Coca-Cola stand to Chairman of the Chemical Division of a Fortune 500 company, he lives, breathes and teaches honorable and effective sales skills.

As a sales representative for Zep Manufacturing Company, Harry was so successful he was named the company's first director of sales. Later, as president of Zep, he led 2,000 salespeople who produced double-digit growth for 25 straight years.

Proud that he has "failed retirement," Harry thinks that selling is something from which you never retire. Today, he is a principal in Southtowne Automotive Group, a successful group of auto dealerships in metro Atlanta, Georgia.

Harry was the first Executive in Residence at Kennesaw State University, where he serves on the board and is active in their highly respected Center for Professional Selling. He serves or has served on several for-profit and civic boards, including the Chemical Specialties Manufacturers Association, the Marcus Jewish Community Center of Atlanta, Junior Achievement, the Atlanta Human Society and the United Way of Metropolitan Atlanta.

Articles by and about Harry have appeared in the *Atlanta Business Chronicle*. In addition, each week for 27 years, Harry wrote an informational and motivational sales letter for his team at Zep Manufacturing.

Harry has a Bachelor of Business Administration degree from Georgia State University. He is a lifelong native of Atlanta, Georgia. He has been married to Sherry for six decades, and together they have three married children and America's eight greatest grandchildren.

END NOTES

[i] The American Legion 138 (Mar. 1995): n. pag. Print.

[ii] Nightingale, Earl. "The Farmer and the Preacher." *Nightingale-Conant*. Nightingale-Conant Corporation, 2013. Web. 3 May 2016.

[iii] *Richard Brannon's Notebook*, Vol. One, copyright 1966, published by Notebook Publications, Columbia, S.C.

[iv] Prentis, H.W., Jr. Editorial. *Daily Standard* 26 Apr. 1977:2.

Newspapers.com The Daily Standard. Web. 6 May 2016.

[v] Raudsepp, Eugene. "The Art of Listening Well." *Inc.com*. Inc Magazine, 1 Oct. 1981. Web. 19 May 2016.

[vi] Mackay, Harvey. "Chasing a Dream? The Only Way to Succeed Is to Commit." *The Business Journals*. The Business Journals, 31 May 2013. Web. 12 May 2016.

[vii] McCall, Morgan W. *High Flyers: Developing the Next Generation of Leaders*. Boston, Mass.: Harvard Business School, 1998. 63. Print.

[viii] Boger, Charles E., ed. "Luck." *The Uplift* (1920): n. pag.

Archive.org. Web. 16 May 2016.

[ix] Covey, Stephen R. *The 8th Habit: From Effectiveness to Greatness*. New York: Free, 2005. 274. Print.

[x] Prentis, H.W., Jr. Editorial. *Daily Standard* 26 Apr. 1977:2.

Newspapers.com The Daily Standard. Web. 6 May 2016.

[xi] *The San Saba Star* 7 Mar. 1966:1. *Newspapers.com* Web. 12 June 2016.

The only people to get even with are those who have helped you.

9 781683 504108